hedgerow #143

a journal of small poems

edited by Caroline Skanne

ISBN: 9798861386456

published by:
wildflower poetry press

www.wildflowerpoetrypress.com

hedgerowhaiku.com

cover photograph 'meadow buttercup' & design: Caroline Skanne
editor: Caroline Skanne

hedgerow is a short-poetry journal dedicated to publishing an eclectic mix of new and established voices across the spectrum of the short poem, with particular attention to English-language haiku & related works.

As always, while submissions are read on a rolling basis, submission reminders are emailed out ahead of each issue. If you are not currently on the mailing list, simply send an email with the subject heading 'subscribe' to:

hedgerowsubmission@gmail.co

dawn breaking birds of the caesura

twilight mark all as read

Cherie Hunter Day

morning
sun

seeps

through
our
sheers

our
every

pore

last days here
a few clouds drifting
toward the mountains

Chuck Brickley

no deer this evening
only their trace
in the long grass

summer heat
the spread of waterlilies
on the lake

Erica Ison

a book
on his belly
the hammock still

goldenrod
the shadow
of a rusted truck

dead swan
floating on the pond
a circle of down

Brad Bennett

peonies
perfume the new moon
shortest night

artist's archive
tucked between clean sheets
a nude sketch

fledgling titmouse
the kid's attempt
to whistle

Kristen Lindquist

house finch—
the rest of his song
flies with him

rising up
from our ancestors' graves
cicada nymphs

Mark Forrester

windfall cleaning up after the grackles

lupines bluing the field bluing the pond

Anne Elise Burgevin

summer meadows
cycling through
lark song

Ingrid Baluchi

beachcombing . . .
the sea spray turns
into a rainbow

Frank Williams

cape light
the crisp edge
of dune grass shadows

Jay Friedenberg

summer twilight
a moth flies
in the shade of poppies

Eufemia Griffo

long summer . . .
the creaking neck
of the electric fan

coastal walk
the cliff
inside

Rob Scott

downwind
from the taffy shop
sea thrift

afternoon sunshine
the cloud
of my desk

Tanya McDonald

the last flicker
of the last candle
a raven's kraa

Eric Sundquist

rainy Sunday the Mexican lily opens red

Domhnach báistiúil osclaíonn an lile Mheicsiceach dearg
(Irish transl. by the poet)

Maeve O'Sullivan

basket willow
a rook's nest
in the tractor seat

four a.m.
night-blooming jasmine
all the way upstairs

chad henry

wherein midsummer fire ants

wind gusts a swirl of shorebirds

Beverly Acuff Momoi

under the willow
. . . the play of light
across her body

Clive Bennett

midsummer
I squeeze myself
between the flowers

if I never
see the Alps . . .
summer clouds

Tony Williams

cottonwood fluff
a breeze moves
the story along

Sharon Martina

a lion's mane jelly
still in the sand
day moon

Joshua St. Claire

so far
just the sound of it
thunder in the valley

Ben Gaa

blood oranges
perfectly quartered
midsummer

Bri Bruce

bright sun
skinny-dipping
in a grotto

Barbara Anna Gaiardoni

reading Bashō
the laundry
can wait

Wilda Morris

mountain wind . . .
a Luna moth's journey
between stars

Jacob D. Salzer

anniversary . . .
sweeping up
dead leaves

Earl Livings

buried
among pink violets
the fallen nestling

Sharon Rhutasel-Jones

after the funeral—
through evening mist the moon
in the corner of her room

Deborah A. Bennett

morning light
streaks of crow across
a white wall

Sarah Paris

Sunday
mass
shooting

Marianne Paul

orange sky . . .
smoke of a distant fire
fills Central Park

Rob McKinnon

a hearse passing by
just like that
blossoms falling

cold night . . .
recalling my inability
to forgive

John Gonzalez

summers end
the mockingbird that never . . .
                    stops

Dyana Basist

the cooling of the day
terns trace thermals
around the faint moon

warbler song
the creek reflects
pine green

a steady wind
across the tarn
starflowers

the beached hulk
of the old wreck
fog tendrils

a snowy egret
dunks and shivers
first light

Hannah Mahoney

Circling Back

Our generation grew up on some legendary cartoons—*Dexter's Laboratory*, *Powerpuff Girls*, *Rugrats*—but today's might be better. In one episode of *Bluey*, in which the characters are dogs, the younger sister makes peace with sickness as a fact of life while stuck in hospital. In another, the older sister peppers her father with questions while en route to the dump, and it's not until she asks him where she was before she was born that he's stumped. Later, when she gets sad upon learning some of her old drawings are being dropped off at said dump, her dad explains that in fact they're being recycled, and that as a result other children will have something to draw on, too.

russet dusk
the blacktail deer leaps
over the hedge

Evan Vandermeer

A New Unknown

I walk down the skyway onto the aircraft, settle into a window seat and watch workers de-ice the wings. Emptying my mind of all things relevant, I ignore the woman beside me who wants to talk and try not to cry. Twenty-eight isn't a bad age unless you don't care if you see twenty-nine.

    daydream
    finding the way between
    then and now

Barbara Tate Sayre

On Pilgrimage

I'm walking along the coastal path towards Spain, and although I've no intention of going to Spain this afternoon, it's pleasant to think that I could. I could cross the Minho River by catching a ferry although I've never done that before, usually entering Spain at Valença by car. I already know where I'll have lunch in Vigo, at a place that does great baby scallops. I'm now on a gastronomic pilgrimage that will end in Santiago de Compostela, where I'll order mussels and a bottle of Alvariño. Later, when my wife picks me up in Caminha—I'm nursing a beer and a couple blisters in a café with a view of Spain across the river—she asks me what I was thinking. I suggest dinner in Vigo.

cold-snap a manhole cover rattling a dream

Bob Lucky

time…I measure it
in morning glories
marigolds…migrations
…falling leaves
jade green rocks found
at Big Sur after eons
in the sea

Carole Johnston

the colour

of evening
from
your porch

your breath
so quiet

ai li

new meds
and my handwriting
gone all to hell—
painfully and slowly
I forge my own signature

Larry Kimmel

there's a place
full of secrets
never shared
driftwood and kelp
on an island shore

Joanna Ashwell

a crack
in the sidewalk—
the get-well card
to mother
never sent

petro c. k.

the things
I manage to do
in this dreamscape
the restful night's sleep
at the bottom of a lake

Cherie Hunter Day

november rain
listening
to it
with
my old cat

night train
night rain
i hear
the rest
of my life

ai li

evening
bleeds into the sea
the first stars
throb into being
alone

Robert Witmer

the sea, the sea
& the way of the whale
waves of memory
waves
of song

the sky open
like the wings of a heron
I stand here
somewhere
between everything & everything

A A Marcoff

ebb tide
boats settle
into the mud

Rober Davey

Indian summer
the old cat's litter
of one

Julie Schwerin

her black eye
a newspaper swollen
with rain

Lorraine Haig

night swim . . .
cicadas above
and underwater

Rick Tarquinio

birdsong my life as an assassin

heat haze
the illusion of beginnings
and ends

Kelly Moyer

half-moon night—
the secret she took
to the grave

power outage—
our argument dissolves
into darkness

Carole MacRury

place of birth—
no more flowers
on dad's roses

Katja Fox

snow eating fruit from a distant season

Alan Peat

funeral day
the slow grating
of coconuts

Matthew Caretti

morning fog
a trail of clothes
leading to the lake

one by one
the shadow
of each ladder
left in the orchard
sunrise

Joseph P. Wechselberger

birdsong motley
making three-bean chili
by feel

shif-
     ting
     weight
     to
     spare
     it
     the
   spi-
der

star frost
a tattered bundle
for a pillow

Evan Vandermeer

new prescription
the black dog pads
towards a patch of sun

Benedict Grant

dusk deepens
the silence
between each breath

Jo McInerney

New Year's Day
full-with-child unfolding
crib instructions

Randy Brooks

sorting through
the wind's effects
preening swallow

Jonathan Humphrey

hospice garden a red leaf sails over the wall

Sheila Windsor

from the bench
some time to consider
a long life

Tom Clausen

spanish steps
          her legs
longer now

Jamie Wimberly

the sea's motion
you rise and fall on the tips
of your toes

David Gale

clacking dominoes
under a coconut palm
slats of shade

Bill Cooper

sunset lake
gathered geese call down
the stragglers

Michele L. Harvey

night-long vigil ribbons of smoke bend through first light

deepening mauve of lilacs—

chaffinches only a sound

Almila Dükel

grappling
with the ancient language . . .
grandmother's prayer book

Madhuri Pillai

country mailbox
a caterpillar
and other news

Pat Davis

dark rows of office windows
the season's first
snowfall

lets us stay
where we are
steady rain

Gary Hotham

a white jug
of red roses
you're back

Christine Eales

sap season
the barman pulls
a pint

John Pappas

labyrinth
the center has gone
to seed

Victor Ortiz

silence
except
a wave

sopping wet
hands outstretched
to starlight

David Kāwika Eyre

abandoned
in a silent street
a child's toy theatre

Christmas Eve
the sound of sellotape
behind a closed door

Liam Carson

the last
of her childhood
windflowers

Kathryn Liebowitz

slow drizzle
bracken faintly scents
the bog's darkness

ragged robin
the quiet child
finds a voice

Thomas Powell

summer morning
a page earmarked
for later

Ella Aboutboul

currawong call
I pause on a river rock
to watch the torrent

Meg Arnot

loosening
an apology
thistledown

Meredith Ackroyd

prairie sunset
cattails catching
the last light

Sharon Martina

first frost folding candied lemon into the dough

P. H. Fischer

perfectly cut stems
in the kitchen sink
Mother's Day

David Grayson

shadows
and light
young maple tree

Iliyana Stoyanova

city stargazing
a tall building hides
Orion's sword

wild strawberries
he returns home
empty-handed

th. vandergrau

midsummer morning
the for sale sign
half light half shadow

Diana Webb

a distant shrill
from an unknown bird
then the rain

starting over
I draw my chair closer
to the fire

Mike Stinson

minor chords
from a tenor sax
blue hour

a lucky slice
of wedding cake
almond blossoms

Marietta McGregor

spring sun—
a teen riding a lawn chair
on a Segway

Marshall Bood

tall grasses wave
in the wind before rain
a curlew's call

James Gilbert

killing frost . . .
arthritic fingers stumble
through a Bach fugue

Roland Packer

snowmelt
the roar
of spring peepers

Laurie D. Morrissey

looking into
more summer kigo
   silent rain

verdure wind
echo of a tennis rally
from the hilltop school

Keiko Izawa

moonrise

answering
   the unasked question

Bill Merk

thunderclap
the sudden chatter
of roosting sparrows

Jennifer Burd

summer's end:
fish around my feet
at Archirondel

Herb Tate

sharper
through the hagstone
the dying sun

Laura Webb

the lacewings
we nearly missed . . .
wild mint patch

Debbie Strange

all the times I meant to visit an old friend's funeral

Royal Baysinger

my father, dying—
sun glints on the nail
a painting hung from

at the peak
what's not rock is
rooted in rock

Peter Yovu

oystercatchers
a young child lets go
of her mother's hand

far out west
kangaroos disappear
with a total eclipse

Ron C. Moss

deer in the yard
who said they were
my zinnias

Laszlo Slomovits

access visit the paper dolls linked together

thawing mountain lake
the beer can
upends

ammonite
a child
guessing its age

empty church
relighting
someone's candle

frances angela

mom's will unfolding night jasmine

Hifsa Ashraf

snow-capped peaks
antlers cupping
blue sky

Claire Vogel Camargo

Alexa's
definition of loneliness
—long afternoon

j rap

I return to thinking
of things I did—
early autumn wind

common grass-pink
where the pine savanna ends—
our map abandoned

Rebecca Lilly

ending
three days of rain
a nuthatch's call

snowmelt
the things I've learned
about moving on

abandoned farm fields of butterflies

Bryan Rickert

ISBN: 9798861386456

published by:
wildflower poetry press

www.wildflowerpoetrypress.com

hedgerowhaiku.com

cover photograph 'meadow buttercup' & design: Caroline Skanne
editor: Caroline Skanne

hedgerow is a short poetry journal dedicated to publishing an eclectic mix of new and established voices across the spectrum of the short poem, with particular attention to English-language haiku & related works.

As always, while submissions are read on a rolling basis, submission reminders are emailed out ahead of each issue. If you are not currently on the mailing list, simply send an email with the subject heading 'subscribe' to:

hedgerowsubmission@gmail.co

Printed in Dunstable, United Kingdom

67204113R00025